Open Secrets:
The Ultimate Guide
to Marketing Your Book

Open Secrets:
The Ultimate Guide to Marketing Your Book

Tupelo Press

Tupelo Press

2021

Open Secrets: The Ultimate Guide to Marketing Your Book
Copyright © 2021 Tupelo Press. All rights reserved.

Library of Congress Catalog-in-Publication data available upon request.

Tupelo Press
P.O. Box 1767
North Adams, Massachusetts 01247
(413) 664-9611 / Fax: (413) 664-9711
editor@tupelopress.org / www.tupelopress.org

Tupelo Press is an award-winning independent literary press that publishes fine fiction, nonfiction, and poetry in books that are a joy to hold as well as read. Tupelo Press is a registered 501(c)(3) nonprofit organization, and we rely on public support to carry out our mission of publishing extraordinary work that may be outside the realm of the large commercial publishers. Financial donations are welcome and are tax deductible.

23 22 21 1 2 3
First printing: May 2021

ISBN 978-1-946482-57-0
Design by Brian Prendergast, Brian P. Graphic Arts

The Tupelo Press Team
Jeffrey Levine, *Publisher & Artistic Director*
Kristina Marie Darling, *Editor-in-Chief*
David Rossitter, *Managing Editor*
Alan Berolzheimer, *Editor-at-Large*
Kirsten Miles, *Director 30/30 Project; Coordinator, Tupelo Press Seminars*
Cassandra Cleghorn, *Poetry Editor and Associate Editor for Nonfiction*
Laurie Sheck, *Fiction Editor*
Sara Veglahn, *Fiction Editor*
Xu Xi, *Fiction Editor-at-Large*
EJ Colen, *Nonfiction Editor*
Allison O'Keefe, *Operations Administrator*
Jacob Valenti, *Operations Administrator*
Hannah Snell, *Marketing Associate*
Emily Breunig, *Fulfillment Coordinator*

CONTENTS

INTRODUCTION

Marketing Your Book

All authors have a vested interest in getting their book into the hands of as many readers as possible. Though it is a publisher's role to aid you as an author and to assist in marketing and publicity for all your books, the purpose of this guide is to prepare you to take the all-important lead in your own marketing. Nobody else can do this essential work for you. This marketing guide is designed to help you make a success of your book. It's jam-packed with the essential tools, ideas, and resources you'll need to achieve that goal.

Jeffrey Levine | *Publisher, Tupelo Press*

Both large commercial and small independent publishing houses strive to spend their limited resources creating books with the highest possible production values. But truth be told, as the author of one of those books, you are the one best qualified, best able, and best positioned to ensure its spread among the widest audience, even if your publisher is one of the most well-resourced commercial presses in the land. Books succeed only when authors work hard to make success a reality. Remember: an independent publisher's continuity is determined solely by the success of its books, which means that they are just as interested in selling your book as you are. Publishers are here to work with you, and will. Here at Tupelo Press, this marketing handbook represents our concerted, joint effort to launch your book toward the success it deserves.

We encourage you to thoroughly and joyfully embrace the notion of self-promotion, knowing that it's the book—your book—that you're breathing life into. You wouldn't have written and published your book if you didn't believe in it, and in yourself, as a writer with important artistic talent. Your publisher believes in you. Your family and friends believe in you. Your current readers believe in you. And future readers will believe in you.

As a strategic playbook, this guide draws upon the ideas and considerable experience of Tupelo Press's editorial and marketing staff.

CHAPTER ONE

Publishing and Book Promotion

Most emerging writers—particularly those creating poetry, short fiction, experimental fiction, and creative nonfiction—find publication through small presses that frequently lack the resources to fully promote their authors in today's competitive marketplace. A writer's involvement in tours, local readings, and other marketing programs in partnership with her publisher can mean the difference between a successfully published book and one that has been merely printed.

CLMP Monograph, "Maximizing the Visibility of Emerging Writers" (2009)

Self-promotion does not mean second-rate promotion. It means that you, as the author, are actively involved in generating the audience acclaim that will ensure success for your book. If your aim is to create a dedicated readership, active and effective self-promotion can be just as powerful as the impersonal advertising campaigns of large publishers. This handbook covers a wide range of book marketing and publicity techniques, emphasizing the role of the Internet, local communities, personal and professional connections, and a host of other publicity tactics. But it all starts with you and your motivation: Successful self-promotion builds off the confidence you have in yourself as a writer and in your book, both as a unique and marketable work of art.

Your publisher is there to help you. While there are limits to how much a small press can do, which is one reason why it is so critical to practice the methods outlined here, an open channel of communication between author and publisher will go a long way toward making your publishing experience more enjoyable and fruitful. The success of your publisher depends upon the success of the authors it publishes. It is in their best interest to do everything they can to help their authors.

Don't feel intimidated by this process; as the author of a new book, you know more about its merits than anyone. You are the best salesperson for your book. And as one who has made the sacrifices necessary to write, edit, and publish a work of literature, you possess a deep reserve of confidence to draw upon when bringing your work to the public.

After a quick overview of the essentials, the following chapters outline three basic categories of book marketing strategy: the means by which you present yourself as an author, or, **The Author's Image**; how you, as an individual, can make headway into what publishers call **The Industry**; and, finally, **The Publisher's Role** in all proceedings.

Planning and Pacing

If you fail to plan, you plan to fail, the saying goes. Self-promotion requires that you spread your attention between many different activities and venues, but by failing to organize yourself, you will exhaust those efforts without achieving significant progress.

Start small. Later, this guide will detail larger advertising strategies, but for now, it is important to imagine how you can connect with others and find a niche in the market on your own terms. Though self-promotion doesn't require a large budget, it will be helpful if you can organize funds to dedicate to marketing. Finding creative ways to use this money will ensure that it goes a long way. Don't be afraid of planners, whiteboards, or spreadsheets—whatever organizational methods you start to employ now will be crucial later in the process. Tupelo Press (or your publisher) may also have resources to dedicate to your budget and organization (see Chapter Four, **The Publisher's Role**).

Part of planning is how you want to present your work to its audience. Take time to think about what makes your book stand out as a unique work, as something exceptional and original. Articulating the distinctiveness of your book will help you to determine your target audience. Once you know your audience, or at least have a sense of a possible audience, you can start to devise targeted marketing tactics.

Marketing also requires a long-term approach. Nothing compares to the excitement of launching your book, but for most writers, successes don't occur overnight. Often, book sales will peak after the initial excitement of its publication dies down because it takes a while for word-of-mouth marketing to make its rounds. Don't get discouraged or disheartened; your book will experience ups and downs during the marketing cycle, and just because it's not doing well for a time does not mean you should give up on marketing.

Instead, you must plan sustainable marketing strategies. To ensure the continued success of your book, you must be committed well before and well after publication. Set goals for your book and don't stop until you achieve them. Maintain a consistent, day-by-day approach for your marketing strategies that you continue for an extended period.

Building a platform is essential for developing a dedicated readership. Spend time building an audience through blogging and social media activity. Use strategies that create enough buzz to get people talking before the book's initial publication, then do your best to make sure those word-of-mouth endorsements spread and keep your book in people's minds.

For now, think of marketing as a to-do list. Start with tasks you can accomplish quickly (like determining a target audience), then follow with items that work best over a long period of time (like following up with word of mouth or consulting bookstores and reviewers). Get in the habit of checking the websites and stores where your book is available. See what kind of criticisms are being made in reviews and if there's anything you can do to respond to them. Don't stress if you can't think of everything right now—the point of this handbook is to provide you with the kinds of strategies you will later use. For now, you just need to be ready to organize them.

Developing an effective plan to discover, develop, and market specifically to your audience will be the easiest way to ensure your success as an author. For now, you need to start thinking in terms of short-term, day-to-day tactics (social media, blogging, and other everyday word-of-mouth techniques) and long-term marketing strategy (events, industry connections, and large-scale advertising campaigns). Although planning and time management will be critical to the marketing process, it is important not to exhaust yourself. Avoid burning out. You must treat every one of your promotional endeavors as equally essential to your end goal. If you spread yourself too thin, it will be obvious to your audience. You only have so much time—choose wisely how you are going to spend it.

If you feel overwhelmed with the number of commitments you have taken on, don't be afraid to back off a bit. Your enthusiasm and motivation are essential, but it's easy to deplete your emotional reserves. Marketing and promoting your book will be difficult at times, and just like writing (or any other form of hard labor), it requires consistency and dedication to accomplish your goals. But take a moment, now and again, to just breathe; remember, the hardest part is over. Your book is complete, and all that remains is to bring it out into the world. Hard work will produce results, but treat yourself well during the time you spend promoting your book. Make sure to practice self-care in ways that nourish your body, mind, and soul.

Knowing Your Work and Audience

Not everybody wants to read your book, and even fewer will pay money for it. Advertising is wasted on readers who do not already possess a desire that advertising can speak to. Instead, you need to define a target audience who already has some level of interest in what you are trying to sell and avoid wasting your time on audiences uninterested in your work. If your book contains adult content, don't try and sell it to a vendor known for its children's books. Conversely, if your book would do well in an academic setting, try marketing to a nearby college or high school by emailing the appropriate departmental faculty or staff.

Know your book's genre and content and use that knowledge as starting points to direct you to your target audience. Associating your book with a genre ensures its identifiable place on store shelves, and not the "miscellaneous" rack in the back corner. Most bookstores, both bricks-and-mortar and online, are organized by genre because that's how most readers buy books. Marketing by genre makes it easier for your audience to find and buy your work.

The composition of your potential audience depends largely on your book's content: Content and audience go hand-in-hand. Ask yourself: Who did you write the book for? How can you best market and connect to your target audience? Spending time getting to know your audience will directly influence sales. Don't just take out an ad in the local paper, instead, take out an ad in a magazine that caters to your niche audience. This is more cost-effective and opens a direct line of contact to your audience, proving you know who they are and where to reach them. Or better, *forget advertising and read the section in this guide on publicity. Publicity is advertising you get for free.* Think like your audience. Research the blogs, websites, and online communities they use to find each other and use the same methods to find markets for your book.

Though bookstores are essential, reaching your target audience might require you to seek out other venues. If your work alludes to or takes place within the African diaspora, for example, you need to be aware of how these connections will influence the available audience and how you can use the content to connect to them. Universities teach and lecture in a broad range of fields and could feature your work in a lecture series or course, where you might find yourself appearing as a guest speaker.

If you have already been published, it's easier to reach out to prospective readers than if you're being published for the first time. You can expand your target audience by examining who has already purchased your book. What communities read your books? What age group attends your events and readings? What ethnicities, occupations, geographical areas, or special-interest groups make up your readership? Take the time to imagine several ways you might reach each of these audiences.

❦ Determining Your Target Market

An author's audience appears as a collection of data. What this means is, in order to have an effective grasp on your target audience, you need to have the data that represents them and learn how to target specific points within it. You can conduct anonymous polling (online or in person) and even gather data on people who attend your author events.

If you've already established an online author presence, Google Analytics is useful for learning more about your audience. Google

Analytics allows you to track visitors to your site for free. You can see where the site traffic came from (i.e., other social media websites) to help you determine which online efforts are most effective. Sometimes, traffic comes from a place you least expect, showing you where to focus your energy in the future.

❦ The Audience for Poetry

The National Opinion Research Center (NORC) at the University of Chicago conducted a study in March 2006 entitled *Poetry in America*, surveying people's attitudes toward and experiences with poetry. It focused on the existing and potential audiences for poetry. including who reads or has read poetry, why they read it, where they read it, and so on. The study found that women, African Americans, young adults between the ages of 18 to 24, and people with graduate degrees are the most likely groups to be part of the existing poetry audience. It indicated that 70 percent of poetry readers have a library card. Overall, it broadly characterizes poetry readers as "active, engaged adults who participate in a variety of leisure and social activities. The current poetry audience reads voraciously with poetry as one of the many genres they enjoy."[1] But frankly, as an independent literary press that has been paying attention to our own metadata for 22 years, we reach different results. We believe that the poetry audience reaches across all age groups from 16 to 98, is not confined to people with advanced degrees, and—depending upon the book—appeals to all races about equally. It may be true that women tend to purchase more poetry than do men, but poetry certainly does appeal to men (in our experience), just as important sectors of our reading audience also include the LGBTQIA+ community, Asian Americans, Latinx, Indigenous, and—perhaps most important—other writers.

❦ The Audience for Fiction

While rates have been declining in recent years, nearly 42 percent of Americans surveyed in 2017 said they were readers of fiction.[2] The audience for fiction is broad and deep, and a wealth of resources about marketing exist on paper, in person, and online for fiction writers. Deepen your relationship with your audience by holding Q&A sessions, readings, and signings. Create an online presence through various author groups and encourage your fans to create a fan club (or if not, create one yourself that they can utilize).

☙ The Academic Audience

It can be challenging to sell your book in academia (meaning course adoptions) given the difficulty of targeting specific professors or universities. If you take this route, you can research trade shows online, find outlets that cater to universities, or attend academic conferences to promote your book. If possible, reach out to professors and teachers you know to recommend your book for a specific course they are teaching. Keep in mind that working with an educational audience is also a marketing process; try and convince them why your book would enhance their course. If they offer the syllabus online, study it and include it in your marketing approach. Write a "Readers Guide" or a "Teachers Guide." Although academic sales traditionally operate on a seasonal schedule (for the fall semester, most professors order books from January to late March, and order for the spring semester from September through late October), professors look for new material all year round. Therefore, reaching out to educators is really a year-round process.

Though challenging, selling to schools can be incredibly lucrative. Making this decision depends primarily on how well your material would translate into course material. Given that college professors have more freedom in their curriculum than K–12 teachers, earning their individual attention will be more valuable. If you are unable to sell your book as part of a course, you may be able to coordinate a reading instead. Look for and target schools that showcase authors and artists through partnerships with local venues.

☙ Your Niche Audience

Remember, the content of your work and your unique expertise as an author will determine what your niche audience looks like. In the absence of focus groups and a demographic analysis department, it is up to you to discover where these individuals meet, how they find each other, and what communities they form. You can discover communities and venues interested in your work by studying their methods and using them to your advantage.

Grassroots Marketing

Successful grassroots marketing requires strategic targeting of scarce resources. As a self-promoter with limited time, energy, and money, you cannot take on the massive audience of global readers head on, but you can seek out communities and attract individual readers by targeting your efforts at a few key locations. This is marketing at the grassroots, the lowest level of public awareness, using local and word-of-mouth tactics that will generate a buzz among underground communities in your area. The next chapter, **The Author's Image**, will expand these efforts to the Internet, where you can use targeted content to reach entire communities and specific subcultures that you would otherwise never encounter. You might not have enough money to buy ads on cable TV networks, but with enough time and adequate preparation, word of mouth can spread just as far and resonate much more intimately with consumers.

At its core, marketing is about forming, keeping, and utilizing relationships. So, what does it look like to apply traditional marketing principles to a grassroots audience? Start by thinking of the relationships you already have: family, friends, coworkers, and special-interest groups, like alumni associations. Bear in mind, you have the power to use all of your relationships to help your book succeed, and forming new connections that will benefit your book is easier than it may seem. Always be on the lookout for ways you can find, contribute to, and nurture these relationships, new and old.

Once you have located yourself within a network of relationships, the best way to spread news about your book is simply by talking about it. Never underestimate the power of word-of-mouth advertising. Studies have found that word-of-mouth promotion is the most effective marketing strategy: the Nielsen Global Survey of Trust in Advertising found that 84 percent of customers are more likely to trust recommendations from friends and family than advertisements (though trust in online advertising is steadily increasing).[3] The American Marketing

Association found in a recent study that 64 percent of marketing executives believe in the power of word of mouth, but only 6 percent claim to have mastered it.[4] In the case of online ads, people are demonstrably more likely to take them seriously if they appear to contain genuine reviews from other customers, which reinforces the evidence that people are more likely to trust others' testimony.[5] You should talk to friends in order to generate word-of-mouth excitement, then go beyond your immediate circle and hone in on less obvious contacts who are likely to endorse your book.

Word of mouth is effective because it starts a chain reaction. The people you promote yourself to are more likely to buy your book and continue to promote it for you. As booksellers will tell you, books are sold by word of mouth. Think about the way that social media (Facebook, Instagram, Twitter, Tik Tok) substitute for word of mouth today. Still, you shouldn't aggressively and desperately try to get ahold of readers—your approach is important. People prefer honesty and engagement from individuals they can relate to. That means you should never force your work into a conversation, but let it come up naturally. If you feel there is an appropriate opportunity, go for it. Gertrude Stein wrote, "You look ridiculous if you dance. You look ridiculous if you don't dance. So you might as well dance."[6] If there is an opportunity to incorporate your book into a conversation, why not take it? It's entirely possible to do so without seeming like a door-to-door encyclopedia salesperson. Just be confident you are bringing up your book in a way that feels natural to you and in the given situation, to avoid overwhelming or annoying your potential reader.

Go through your phone contacts or address book and ask yourself who would have a genuine interest in your book. Try your best to reach out to people who are not only interested in your work, but are interested in promoting and praising it to others. Give these trusted readers copies of your book and keep them informed and up to date about its progress. Actively involve those around you with the subject matter of your book by providing them with any exciting news or current events related to it.

Relationships, whether online or off, take time to build, and they are the crux of your marketing efforts, so don't wait until your book is coming out to start promoting it. You need to find and attract your audience long before your book is on shelves. As your book makes its way through the editorial and production processes, start thinking about how you're going to sell and who is going to buy. Use the publishing process as a time to develop a plan of action for your book's release to stimulate interest in your readers.

Generating excitement around your book will take time and effort. Most importantly, you should keep your audience up to date. Experiment with different formats, like email, snail mail, social media, and phone calls. These marketing approaches cost next to nothing, so try out each and see which agree most with you or seem to be most effective in reaching your audience. Strive to keep a constant buzz surrounding your book to prove its worth to your audience, reviewers, and others. Use these resources to maintain contact and sustain your book's relevance, and you will be even more successful.

Even the publication of your book does not mean the conversation has to stop. There is no set time during which your book is relevant; books published in the past ten or fifteen years are still being aggressively marketed right now. Usually, your publisher will market your book for four months leading up to the book's release and typically for about a year afterwards (we do at Tupelo Press). After that, it's up to you if you want to continue marketing, and with inexpensive grassroots marketing techniques, there's little reason to not continue; your grassroots marketing network can only expand.

CHAPTER TWO

The Author's Image

I n the twenty-first century, producers and consumers don't always directly interact. Now with an abundance of information online, nothing is more powerful than a coordinated body of information that portrays you, the author, in an appealing light. The following sections explore how this information reaches your audience, and how you can target specific individuals and communities who are likely to enjoy your work. Though they mainly focus on the Internet, these techniques will also apply to all your in-person efforts and interactions. If advertising is all about the exchange of information, effectively distributing quality information about your image will lead to sales and success.

You Are the Best Salesperson for Your Book

Never forget, as the author, you are your book's best salesperson. You may have qualms about packaging your image as a brand, and spending so much time trying to get readers to purchase your book might begin to feel manipulative or disingenuous. Literature shouldn't be about a bottom line, and most small presses absolutely respect that.

But you still want your book to succeed, and for a literary or academic press to continue sharing great writing with the world, it needs an audience to keep afloat. You can do this without engaging in practices you find manipulative or heavy-handed—the practices outlined here specifically allow you to express your genuine passion for the work and its success. If you discover the marketing practices and communities that feel completely natural to you, then you will not only avoid feeling like a PR agent, but you will also connect with an audience you enjoy and find a unique place in the literary landscape.

Branding

Part of being an author today is generating a cloud of information to follow your name wherever people mention it online. In the twentieth century, large companies figured out how to present themselves this way in the physical world through the association of images with objects. Slogans, logos, and the emotional attachments that individuals associate with consumer products are all components of branding. As an author, you won't find yourself engaging in all these practices, but the principle remains the same: Your name should generate a series of associations, both in the consumer's mind and in search engines

To a publishing novice, branding might seem overwhelming and unnecessary, a corporate marketing approach. Although most authors don't think about it (or don't want to), authors need brands, too. Branding functions for authors just as it functions for companies: It gives you name recognition and helps you sell your products (books).

Think back to the planning stage, where you determined the unique aspects of your book that could be potential selling points. Ask yourself again: What makes your book distinct? Make sure you have a clear outline of what this looks like to help you develop the best platform for your brand.

❦ Be Consistent

Make sure that anything you post online or write about in a physical promotion coheres with the branding you have established for your book. Use the same title, tag line, photo, and colors across all branding opportunities. Of course, the more books you write with similar themes or elements, the stronger your brand becomes.

❦ Coordinate with Your Book's Color and Fonts

Chances are your book already has a unique font and color scheme. Use these as a primary design template for your media. Don't make your branding identical in every case, but certainly use different branding opportunities to complement one another. Whether designing promotional bookmarks or website layout, always consider what colors best compliment your primary color scheme.

If you have access to the font used on your book's cover, use that same font as much as you can in promotional materials to take advantage of the familiarity of the brand. If you don't have access to that exact font, try to use whatever font best resembles it. Always keep in mind what makes your book unique, and use that to build your brand.

Judge books by their covers. When it comes to branding, a book's cover is everything. Branding is a matter of both name recognition and visual recognition, and it continues to sell your book by creating a memorable image in readers' minds. Care and focus in essential branding decisions creates a coherent aesthetic, representing you as an author and making you immediately recognizable to your audience.

The Internet: Your Website

Your website is where you are in control. No one else can change the rules like they can on other social media sites. While some players in the publishing industry contend that you can use a social media site in place of having a website, I couldn't disagree more. A website is where you call the shots. If you are only on social media sites, you are always playing another person's game.

Fauzia Burke, "Why Authors Need Websites," via Huffington Post, 2014 [7]

As an author, you need a website that centralizes all the news and information connected to you in a way that you control. The Internet is a major influence in every aspect of our lives: A 2015 Pew Research Center study found that 84 percent of American adults use the Internet.[8] While household income, age, race, gender, community type, and education level all influence Internet use, the fact remains that it is an integral part of our politics, economics, and socialization. The Internet is unavoidable when promoting your book.

Before you begin creating your online persona, you must recognize the importance of keeping your technology up to date. If you don't consider yourself a tech-savvy author, *Author Media.com* offers step-by-step tutorials for creating and maintaining websites, blogs, and social media pages.

Fully utilizing the Internet is about more than simply creating a space for yourself online; the online space you create should be user-friendly, easy to navigate, and current. Your website should be fun, accessible, and thought-provoking for both you and your audience.

❦ Your Website and You

Your website should include information about you not just as an author, but about you as a person. Including personal information both humanizes you and provides meaningful ways for readers to connect with you. Write a small blurb that will function as an "About the Author" for your website and maintain it across all other social media. Be concise and offer a message about who you are and what work you do that coincides with your brand.

❦ Your Website and Your Brand

The importance of branding continues online; your website is an excellent opportunity to expand your brand. Though social media is great for generating a relationship with your readers, it is your website that will give potential readers a clear understanding of you as an author. Your website should reflect—to the best of your ability—your principles and your brand's aesthetic.

Keep your website up to date and accessible, while also maintaining brand consistency. Use color schemes and fonts from previous marketing, updating when necessary. Include taglines and your branding statement to improve audience recognition. Include links to places where readers can buy your book and be sure to highlight important information like upcoming events and contact info. This does not mean that you should throw a bunch of information on the page. Instead, you should make your entire website visually appealing by including images, video clips, and interesting links. Update your page regularly, especially regarding awards, news, or events that relate to you and your book. If you have received some press or made appearances on other sites, provide links.

🍃 Your Website's Design

Entire books have been written about the best ways to build a website. Remember that your website's design should reflect the integrity of your work. Take a minimalist attitude toward design; a website that is too flashy or too crowded is irritating to the eye. Website visitors are there to find out about you and your book—how to purchase it or contact you.

Operate realistically; you're not on an unlimited budget, so don't feel as though you must go all-out in designing the most expensive website on the Internet. WordPress is highly recommended for ease of use, customization, and accessibility for authors' websites. Not only is WordPress relatively user-friendly, its basic options are free, with more utilities and features available at various price levels. We highly recommend adding a custom domain, otherwise you will be stuck with a URL ending in ".wordpress.com." WordPress even allows you to construct your own design template, color scheme, and font. The platform Wix is another good option.

Most importantly, show—don't tell. The old movie director's adage applies just as well to marketing on your website and on social media. Don't just talk about your book, show it. Put up relevant pictures and insert excerpts of your book when applicable. If you feel creative, try generating an image quote, which is your own picture (or a free license image) layered under a particularly powerful quote from your text. Take care that the quote is attributed to you or to your book on the picture, since image quotes tend to go viral. Sometimes quotes are reposted on Twitter, Facebook, Tumblr, hundreds of thousands of times. This kind of marketing might seem too time consuming for something that is not guaranteed to generate any buzz, but it is becoming more common and has proven its effectiveness. Canva, for example, is a website that makes it easy to create attractive image quotes and social media posts on the fly.

🍃 Your Website and Publicity

Ensure that your site comes up in Internet searches. Google and Bing both have features that enable you to submit your website into their search engines. Furthermore, build your website by creating multiple pages, tags, and links to other relevant sites. Keep a blog of updates related to your book and its subject, as blogs are especially great for turning up results in search engines because the content is always updating. Authors with the most dedicated followings update their blogs the most thoroughly and consistently. To keep people coming back to your website, post intentionally and frequently.

Try to make connections with other sites so that a link to yours can be displayed. Conversely, link to other websites, authors, and information related to your book. Cross-promote by posting and sharing works like yours, be it in theme, genre, or other books from your publisher. This way, you establish yourself as a genre expert while also putting your own name out there. It's impossible to know ahead of time what sort of connections you may make by cross-promoting your work—you might end up in dialogue with other authors, new readers, or critics. The more connections you make, the more visitors to your site.

❦ Your Website or Blog and Social Media

In her 2016 book, *Online Marketing for Busy Authors: A Step-by-Step Guide*, Fauzia Burke stresses the urgency and importance of having a professional and cutting-edge website. We would add that maintaining a blog ("weblog") is equally important. Therefore, wherever you see "website," think also, "blog." Burke is the founder and president of FSB Associates, one of the first firms to specialize in digital branding and online publicity. On author websites, Burke writes:

> Your website is the only place online where you are in total control. No one else can change the rules like they can on other social media sites. Other social media platforms don't cancel out the need for a website because your website is where you call the shots. If you are only on social media sites, you are always playing another person's game. You don't want your online presence to be in the hands of someone else.[9]

Acknowledging the importance of social media, Burke argues that you should start conversing with your audience by selecting a platform where you think you will find your readers. You can always adjust accordingly as you build your reading community.

The Internet: Social Media Presence

Your goal should be to establish an influential Internet presence. Not only should fans be able to find and follow you on the Internet, but new associations should be made and new contacts formed. Just like your grassroots presence, you should be available and ready for journalists, interviewers, and publicists to reach you.

When it comes to building a website or a blog, you don't have to unravel the mysteries or go it alone. There are any number of terrific blog- and website-building software providers. Here's where to look for comparisons: https://www.top10bestwebsitebuilders.com/. Each provider will guide you step-by-step through the process. If you have a friend or colleague who can act as a spirit guide, so much the better!

☙ Using Social Media Effectively

As you know full well, the world has entered solidly and irrevocably into the era of social media. If you want your book to succeed, there's no substitute for embracing social media, and there's more useful content on the Web than you can shake a magic wand at. Here's a short run-down of excellent online tools. If you read nothing else in this marketing guide, you'll want to spend a good deal of quality time with these can't-do-without resources, and be sure to coordinate your social marketing strategies with your publisher:

- IngramSpark (a division of Ingram, the largest book wholesaler in the U.S.) provides this useful content, "How to Promote a Book on Social Media: 13 Tips for Indie Authors," https://www.ingram spark.com/blog/7-social-media-tips-for-authors. Spark is Ingram's self-publishing service. While we are not recommending that you self-publish your book, IngramSpark's *marketing advice* is pertinent for all writers, and we suggest that you familiarize yourself fully with their suggestions, no matter what organization has brought your book into being, from the largest commercial publishing house to the smallest micro-press.

- Rachel Thompson, a marketing-savvy writer, offers invaluable advice in "How to Create a Pre-Launch Strategy for Your Book,"

https://medium.com/the-1000-day-mfa/this-is-how-to-create-a
-pre-launch-strategy-for-your-book-a7810ed0da6b.

- We also recommend (from BookMarketingTools.com) "6 Steps for Creating a Social Media Campaign that Drives Your Book Launch," https://bookmarketingtools.com/blog/6-steps-for-creating-a -social-media-campaign-that-drives-your-book-launch/.

- While you're at it, spend some time with "8 Hints on How to Effectively Promote Your Book on Social Media" by Brandon Stanley, found at Nonfictionauthorsassociation.com: https://nonfictionauthors association.com/8-hints-on-how-to-effectively-promote-book -on-social-media-by-brandon-stanley/.

You shouldn't expect more from your fans than you're willing to give. As a creator, you need to realize that social media done well is a matter of quality and timing, availability, and a willingness to provide interesting content.

CREATE NEW OPPORTUNITIES FOR EXPOSURE

Poets should pay particular attention to this detail. The aforementioned *Poetry in America* study found that incidental exposure—coming across a poem in an unplanned manner—broadens audience participation.[10] Adult readers will read poetry when it appears in magazines, on advertisements, and in books. Television, radio, and the Internet, too, present opportunities for more people to read and listen to poetry.

Don't be afraid to post fragments of your work online. Try minimizing the word count to something that will hook readers and make them curious to discover the rest of your work. You could even participate in online literary trends, like "140-character novels" or "six-word stories." A well-written submission or unique use of social media can grab the attention of your audience. On the other hand, this doesn't mean you need to constantly post segments of your work. A good social media site balances the stimulation of new content with the audience's interest and drive for new content.

Use social media to discover other authors or experts in your area who have a similar and slightly larger following than you. This list should comprise professionals, leading thinkers, and experts who are either not quite up to "guru" status or don't have celebrity-sized followings. You want to create this core team so you can use their connections to help promote you and your work. You should seek their advice and, with their permission, link to their posts and share their work as much as possible. Let these fellow genre experts know what you've done. These messages are best when they thank the writer for creating the work in the first place and avoid asking for a link, shout out, or anything else in return. Communicating in this way, though it may feel one-sided, helps fuse the connection—the relationship—with a person in your field. Aside from being a rare gesture on social media, standing out from retweets, comments, and likes, it is practice in giving without demanding compensation. Plus, when it comes time to ask a small favor, you will already have revealed your name and the better side of your personality.

When your social media connections have grown strong enough, ask for a small favor from your fellow authors and experts. Would they be interested in previewing your eBook or product materials? What about a joint venture? Reaching out in a small way can have a big payoff.

QUALITY: BROADEN AND DEEPEN

The breadth of your Internet presence is important; the more websites you use, the easier it is for your audience to reach you. The Internet should be a way for you to interact with more people than you ever could in person. Become a part of many different social media platforms. Experiment with different ways of posting and formatting your content until you find one that suits you. Once you have determined which websites you are comfortable with, make it your goal to provide substance to your Internet presence.

Posting without thought can actively harm your ability to succeed online. Be conscious of your actions online; while connecting with your audience through the Internet, employ the same tact and social awareness that you would in your everyday physical interactions. Don't treat social media as just another marketing opportunity; use it to add to the conversation. To do this, try not to portray yourself as an infallible expert. Instead, open your interactions up to make others feel like experts. Create opportunities for your audience to collaborate, contribute, and share. Even though you use a machine, be a human.

☞ Marketing Tools

Use social media as an additional space for yourself and as a free marketing tool. Social media can allow you to reach a whole new audience that you would not have had access to previously. You can use social media to post work, upcoming events, reviews, and other relevant information, if you keep your pages up to date. A perk about social media is that it makes people feel included—it allows you to engage with your audience and permits them to engage with you and your work more intimately, even if you may not know them personally. What you allow to be public on social media should reflect this and should welcome your audience to be a part of your work. Make sure what you post is a mix of both interests and information, so you not only keep people informed, but you also keep them engaged and more closely connected with you.

MAILING LISTS

Don't underestimate the importance of the mailing list and certainly incorporate the feature into your website. Mailing lists, considered antiquated by some in the age of social media giants, is actually a very effective tool for marketing. Think about how often you check your email.

Be sure to include a link to subscribe to your mailing list on your website. A person on your mailing list is considerably more likely to purchase your new book than someone on other social media, bar none. Your publisher may maintain a mailing list, but we encourage authors to keep their own mailing list as well.

Your mailing list might end up being your most important marketing asset. People are more willing to sign up for emails from you than you may expect. Emailing people with an update reminds them that your book exists, and that's half the battle.

WEBINARS

The appeal of the webinar ("web seminar") is growing. The convenience of something like a book reading or Q&A with an author conducted at a computer is attractive to most people. The success of featurettes like TED Talks and Reddit AMAs ("Ask Me Anythings") indicates a growing interest in online events.

In a webinar, you can speak directly to your audience through an audio or video link to an online service. Although you can purchase several online products and platforms, you have probably used free programs like Google Hangouts, Skype For Business (Basic), and Zoom to host or attend a webinar. As you likely know, online literary events skyrocketed during the Covid-19 pandemic, including author readings, panels, and discussions, proving that online events are an easy way to publicize and market your book from the comfort of your own home.

You don't have to go viral to gain an audience. Sustained efforts to keep small groups of people talking can be just as effective as a viral mainstream campaign. Your ongoing conversation with dedicated readers can quickly evolve into speaking engagements, paid blog posts, and interview opportunities, all of which means increased traffic on your Facebook page and personal website, increasing sales and brand recognition. The most important way to connect with this small but hard-core audience is to sustain the conversation. Think about the actions you can take, every day, to maintain the buzz. Webinars and social media likes are only two easy and accessible strategies.

🍃 Organizing Your Accounts

A quality social media presence requires careful planning. Set aside time each week to cultivate and create relationships on Twitter, Facebook, or Instagram. Try to ask your followers stimulating questions that will encourage them to reach out to you and provide them a space to do the same! As a platform, Facebook is particularly useful for encouraging users to share their everyday lives and personal insights, an aspect of the service you should use to your advantage. Use social media to speak to your audience on their terms, not strictly on yours. You need to ensure that your page is rife with content your fans will return to, content that is not only enjoyable but adds to their social media experience.

For an author, the importance of social media is not only keeping your pages up to date and your audience buzzing, but using it to provide a window into your daily life. Simple updates, like posting about a book you are reading for fun or highlighting a recipe you made for dinner, humanize you to your audience and allow them to connect with you more intimately. You need to fully engage with the social media communities you are part of—while you should focus on your own content, also follow others and comment on what they are sharing. Join relevant subgroups to increase your exposure (and point your fans toward new interests), and make sure that all your social media accounts are linked together so that your followers can share your activity across multiple platforms. Most networks offer space on each profile to list your other accounts and website information.

When you do post an announcement or important update, remember that they usually work best with a hook—whether an image, quote, or memorable icon. Tag your posts for easy searching and so they appear in other feeds that display similar interests, using both general and specific terms to increase the chance of an algorithm picking up your content. Most importantly, make sure the announcement feels like an organic reflection of you and your interests, not just marketing copy.

Here are some tips to help you achieve a cohesive Internet presence across many different platforms:

- **Use the same short paragraph for your "About the Author" blurb across multiple sites.** Your short paragraph should be a concise, focused message about who you are and what work you do.

- **Make effective use of #hashtags.** Hashtags are helpful for organizing your posts and linking you to specific interest groups. They also catalog your content and make it easy for readers to find information about you. Hashtags can offer new modes of audience interaction: As an author, you can put out a call for creative content from your fans by generating a new hashtag. Use them whenever possible, but don't let it go to your head; as a writer and ambassador of the English language, posts riddled with Internet lingo might turn a literary audience away.

- **Link all your social media together.** Your social media presence must represent a coherent effort on a united front. Some fans might follow you on Twitter but not on Facebook and miss a crucial update. Facebook, Twitter, and Tumblr offer master update pages that will post to all your different platforms at once in order to save you time and energy.

- **Generate lists and organize your accounts.** Try to categorize your followers by interest, industry, or field of expertise. Besides dedicated services like TweetDeck, most social media sites offer widgets to automate such tasks.

❦ Amazon

Amazon conducts more than 60 percent of all online book sales, which means establishing a relationship with the behemoth is essential for most authors. But for most authors within independent publishing, the story is a little different: While the market is definitely shifting to reflect the popularity of eBooks, poetry in particular has fared poorly on electronic markets and so far has escaped the demands of online retail services.

Your publisher might send copies of your book to Amazon and other online retailers for you, so the logistics may not be a part of your planning. However, consider these ideas to help market your book using Amazon:

- **Review other books in your niche and display your expertise.** This will give you more credibility as an expert in your field and expose your name to the sort of audience that reads reviews. If you sign your reviews as "_____, *author of* _____," then you will attract future readers by connecting your expertise and opinions to your work.

- **Review the books that compete directly with yours.** Consumers buying these books are already interested in your niche, so it is very likely that they'll look up or accidentally discover your book along the way. This means that, wherever your competitor succeeds, you have attached your name and work, allowing you to ride their wave.

❦ Launching on Amazon

As an author, knowing your way around Amazon, the largest retailer in the world, can help you reach a larger audience and increase sales. Amazon is an essential part of book sales, despite the platform's complicated relationship with publishers.

Consumers are looking for and buying books differently, so you want your book visible and searchable on all platforms. It's essential to build enthusiasm for your book before it's published and launches on Amazon. As this section outlines, you can build excitement and awareness for your book by reaching out to your base audience, getting reviews from your readers on the day of your Amazon launch, and creating sales momentum.

While reaching "bestseller" status on Amazon for a short period of time might be appealing (and it certainly doesn't hurt), you need to figure out what sales strategies work best for your book short and long term. Nevertheless, the following steps are essential practices to raise awareness of your book, and to secure consistent sales in a fickle market. Just like your book launch, you need to prepare ahead of time, maintain momentum post-publication, and reflect on what you could do differently.

AHEAD OF TIME: WHO CAN YOU REACH OUT TO?

1. Everything in this book so far has had you thinking about this: Who is your niche audience? Who wants to read your book, and who will pay money for it?

   Once you have these basic questions answered, reach out to your base audience. If you have built a mailing list, email your contacts. Of course, in addition to emails and word of mouth, use social media to let your followers know when your book is coming out, how they can preorder, and how to write a review.

   Think about your goals, and how many copies you want to sell. What would this look like day-to-day?

2. Gather up your base and reach out to them to let them know how they can help. If you are a first-time author and are still in the process of building your audience, collect your contacts: family, friends, former professors and classmates, and coworkers. While it's nerve-wracking, remember that the people in your life want to see your book do well. Not to mention, it's exciting to be a part of a book launch.

3. Make sure your base audience has access to an ARC (Advance Reader Copy) of your book, either as an e-galley or a physical copy. Prepare your materials ahead of time, and if you're mailing physical ARCs, organize a list and make sure you're sending them out early enough so readers receive them at least a week before your publication date. Of course, when it comes to reaching out to media outlets, coordinate with your publisher.

4. Ask your base to read your book and draft an honest review (you may decide to send along a reader's guide for context to help readers properly engage with your work). Emphasis on *honest*; your goal is engagement and interest, not perfection. Plus, potential readers browsing books on Amazon may not trust a listing with dozens of five-star reviews, void of thoughtful criticism and discussion. Your publisher believes in your book and knows the right readers will love it, too.

   You can also ask your readers to prepare a brief review (a short paragraph would be fine) ahead of time and save it until your book launches. Make sure to check in from time to time and answer any questions; ensure you're engaging with your audience and not just asking for favors.

   In the week or two leading up to your book's Amazon launch, you may want to send a few friendly emails counting down to the release. To make it an equal exchange, send exclusive content. You could share a cover reveal (if applicable), an unboxing video, or a clip of you reading a piece from your book. You can also create posts on your Amazon listing, to drive traffic and engagement. Most likely, not everyone will want to or be able to buy your book, but they might want to support you in other ways. Keep this in mind so you don't get discouraged, but reach out to as many followers as possible, and give people options for how they can help your book launch on Amazon (and other e-commerce sites) succeed.

5. Make sure your book is listed on Amazon. Your publisher will likely be happy to help or post the listing for you. Coordinate

your Amazon strategy with them, as they might have resources and tips available. But, you're also responsible for making sure your book is posted and any bumps are smoothed out before your launch. You can also set up your author profile with a short bio and a headshot using Amazon Author Central (if your publisher hasn't already done so). Making an author profile can significantly increase your book's visibility, so don't overlook this.

Once your book is posted, provide precise keywords and subcategories. Books in specific niche categories are usually easier for readers to find. Don't just label your poetry collection as "poetry," for example. Does it have a spiritual, religious, or cultural component? What themes is it centered around? What ways do form, hybridity, and subgenre make your collection unique? Use these guiding questions to help narrow down the genre(s) your book falls into. Be analytical: Try different keywords and metadata to see what gets traction and what doesn't. You might have to test different keywords every few days. If you're struggling with metadata, your publisher will likely be happy to help.

ON THE DAY OF:

1. Check back in with your followers. Remind them that your book is released today and let them know if they wrote a review, now is the time to post it on Amazon, since it will help with your ranking and visibility. Also, encourage your readers to buy your book, if they can and haven't already. Keep your reminder email short and sweet, and don't forget to thank everyone for their support so far.

2. Offer other ways your followers can support you. Not everyone can post a review on Amazon and some people might choose not to buy from Amazon. Keep this in mind and be patient with yourself and others. Above all, your goal is to increase your book's visibility to help new readers find your book.

Other options include writing a review on Goodreads or NetGalley, (or other e-galley platforms—ask your publisher), or big-box bookstore websites (like Barnes & Noble and Books-A-Million). And never underestimate the power of social media. You could invite your audience to use a hashtag when posting on social media, and share their posts on your social platforms for an extra incentive.

Of course, don't forget to send a big "thank you" to your supporters. Go beyond words and posts and consider holding a giveaway, contest, or impromptu livestream reading; get creative in showing your gratitude. Share and celebrate your success with them, and let them know they are a part of it.

REFLECT:

So, you've just published your book and launched it on Amazon: Congratulations! Take time to reflect on what worked and went well leading up to and during your launch. What tactics worked best? Is your book continuing to sell and/or rank, or are sales stalling? What was the turnout from your supporters like? You may consider exploring other options, like seeking out more reviewers, experimenting with different keywords, or even advertising on Amazon. Maybe the strategy is long term: You might want to reevaluate how you interact with followers on social media or grow your mailing list. Take note of what worked and what didn't on your launch. Critical reflection will help you shift your focus going forward, and perhaps, help with the launch for your next book. Whatever your concerns or thoughts, your publisher is there to help you along the way.

❦ Facebook

Besides collecting followers and posting updates, you can use Facebook to advertise to potential readers. Advertising doesn't guarantee sales, and if you spend too much without seeing an immediate return, you may be discouraged. Start small, working your way toward larger, more aggressive advertising down the road.

Facebook allows you to specify where your ads will be most relevant. It allows you to tailor your ads to the user's device and location on the page. Direct, targeted advertisements are an excellent opportunity to reach a niche audience, so consider branching out and exploring other advertising services (Google AdSense is ubiquitous) but beware the personal investment that it requires.

Short of targeted ads, Facebook also offers several other unique ways to interact with your readers:

- Offer a contest for a signed copy of your book that will generate buzz for your work.

- Post articles and videos directly relevant to your book, including anything you are involved with. If you do an interview on a podcast or radio show, encourage them to post it so you can link directly to it on your page. Or, with their permission, upload it yourself to a YouTube or Soundcloud account for easier access.

- If you keep a personal blog on your website, Facebook is a useful place to recycle those blogs as status updates. While your personal website should always act as home base, not everyone is going to look at it—some people might only get as far as your Facebook page, which makes it a good place to repost a lot of your website content, or link back to your website.

- Don't assume that everyone knows about your book. Although it makes up a large part of your life, and the Facebook profile you've been building does everything to emphasize you as an author, post reminders about your work consistently (but modestly). People forget, and others might like your page but miss the fact that you have a new book.

- Create a Facebook group about your book. This will allow you to interact with your readers regularly, even daily, and provides another platform from which to promote your work.

Sites and Communities to Explore

Most readers (and writers) imagine that writers are introverts and recluses. Whether or not this is true (and, well . . .), being active on social media among grassroots communities is key for author success. The intimacy of grassroots networks makes readers perceptive, savvy, and vocal, and allows them to exercise unprecedented freedom of taste. But more than anything, readers are less afraid than ever to call out the fake and disingenuous among them. In order to gain trust and a loyal following, you must develop a genuine and heartfelt interest in these communities and consistently interact with them. It's easy to discover platforms you would use naturally, whether mainstream or obscure, and to maintain them in the same way you maintain your work.

☞ Other Websites to Consider

Go beyond your base website and social media. A few websites to look into for getting the word out about your book include (but are not limited to):

- **Tumblr**—A blogging platform that caters to the sort of people who might love to discover an unread novel.

- **Goodreads**—The ultimate site for bookworms on the Internet; naturally a great place to market your book. Make sure you have both an author and a book page on this website.

- **Reddit.com/r/books & Reddit.com/r/literature**—Reddit, self-proclaimed "Front Page of the Internet," offers an "Ask Me Anything" for authors on both of their major book-related subreddits (and you can start your own).

- **YouTube**—YouTube's underbelly boasts a vibrant, if fragmented, literati. These are "early adoption" communities—actively avoiding widespread trends, they are eager to discover new and obscure content. The video platform is also home to the BookTube community, full of enthusiastic book reviewers—a great opportunity for influencer marketing.

- **Instagram**—Pictures of your book with some carefully chosen hashtags tell a story, and storytelling can be a surprisingly effective marketing device. Instagram literature accounts offer an established outlet, but also look to flash fiction contests and other visually appealing accounts. Like YouTube's BookTube, Instagram boasts a large Bookstagram community full of reviewers happy to receive advance copies of books.

- **Review Sites**—BookThing, Bookish, BookLike, Shelfari, and Net-Galley are all very popular review websites for reading and collection curation.

- **Marketlist.com**—With a space for authors to self-promote, the Market List is a tool for writers to connect to magazines, book publishers, agents, writing contests, and websites.

- **National Novel Writing Month, nanowrimo.org**—During the month of November, the NaNoWriMo challenge draws hundreds of thousands of writers determined to write 50,000 words in a month. The site allows you to track your progress and connect with fellow participants.

- **101 Websites for Writers**—From *Writer's Digest*, Kara Gebhart Uhl's list is a resource for writers to determine where and how to best spend their time on the Internet. Organized into eight sections, the guide offers resources in creativity, writing advice, agents, marketing, jobs, online communities, and genres/niches.

CHAPTER THREE

The Industry

S o far, this guide has primarily focused on what you can do as an individual to connect to other individuals—through your author image, brand, and involvement with online communities. But there's another side to marketing that goes beyond reaching people and selling yourself book by book, a side of the business that requires you to enter the industry mainstream. For an individual, this is not always an easy task, and there's a reason why earlier sections focus so heavily on individual self-promotion, where your efforts will come to the greatest fruition. However, long-term efforts sometimes require a broader scope, and with the right combination of timing, targeting, and social presence, you can find your place in the mainstream literary consciousness.

Publicity

Previous chapters covered how you can generate a buzz within niche communities and among networks of individuals online, but there is still great power in traditional media. Because you're not yet an established author, you will have to approach these outlets in the same way you approached the online communities, but the end result will be somewhat different. Instead of making personal connections with individual readers to spread the news of your book by word of mouth, you'll be trying to get your book reviewed or win an award to reach a larger target audience.

❦ Reviews and Awards

Trying to get your book reviewed by a major publication will mean facing widespread competition. Although it's worth it, consider seeking sites, publications, or even individual reviewers who are hungry for new content within your niche. Target your search to the same parameters that determine your core audience—but feel free to think a little larger here. Instead of trying to pin down a hard-core audience that will support your work over time, think of large-scale reviews as a kind of advertising scattershot: loosely targeted, effective for a short period of time, but likely to hit a wider audience than usual.

Awards operate on a slightly different principle, in which the best strategy is to seek out the most highly coveted awards. Avoiding competition by seeking out smaller awards may work in the short term, but piling awards and honors next to your name without the substance to back them up risks appearing over-branded and pretentious to your audience. Seeking out one or two awards connected to your audience and their interests will prevent you from spreading your content too thin or facing competition from too wide a pool of authors.

❦ Advertising Campaigns and Other Publicity Options

Chapter 2, pages 29–30, covers Facebook advertising campaigns. But why stop there? Though it requires a large investment of money, and will not be feasible for most new authors, consider taking out advertisements in physical and/or online publications. This is not a practice to take lightly, and it doesn't make sense to divert funds you have already planned to use elsewhere, as it can very quickly leach money from the funds you've set aside for traveling and otherwise promoting your book. However, a successful ad in a physical publication will reach a much wider audience than you could ever hope to cover by word of mouth or speaking engagements in such a short period of time.

There are many other ways to engage in large-scale publicity—this section is only a basic overview of the possibilities. For larger projects, it's best to consult with your publisher before moving forward, as they have access to many of the resources listed above and can help you manage the process from their end. For more on how your press can help you with this part of the process, see Chapter 4, **The Publisher's Role**.

Events and Industry Connections

"Industry" is a somewhat abstract term—it can refer to individuals within the business, to a group of major corporations and companies, or to any events, publications, and locations that bring these groups together. This section will focus on how to navigate the world of physical interaction with professionals by going to the places where you are likely to find them. Talking over the phone beats an email conversation—but a handshake and a smile has the potential to open a relationship worth as much as an entire advertising campaign.

❦ Trade Shows

- Go to the major book shows and trade shows, or (if you want to compete with fewer authors) to smaller regional conventions and shows. The regional shows are often more cost-effective, but will obviously reach a smaller audience.

- At the shows, make sure you are prepared to take orders for your book, offer special discounts, and have catalogs and brochures ready to distribute. If you have new books, put them on display.

- Use the shows to make new contacts—marketing contacts, like buyers and wholesalers, but also media contacts. Trade shows also offer an opportunity to meet other authors and publishers.

- Above all, make sure your book is visible!

❦ Organizing Events

- You are perfectly capable of independently arranging events and signings; just be sure to coordinate your efforts with your publisher, to make the events as effective as possible.

- Work with local opportunities first, searching for outfits that do the best job of promoting their events.

- Give the store enough time for publicity and promotion. Bookstores typically require two or three months advance notice.

- Make sure you also publicize your event through all your media outlets. Put it on your website, and make sure your publisher knows how to update their own media contacts. Don't forget to see if the location itself has media contacts who can publicize the event.

- Besides readings and signings, you can also set up other types of events that may relate to your book—try hosting events in places like art galleries, libraries, and restaurants.

- If you think your book would sell well somewhere other than a bookstore, reach out.

- If it would reach your audience, you can visit schools and colleges to promote your book and engage with readers.

❦ Readings

- Appearing at a venue has an immense impact on marketing appeal. While we've talked a lot about posting online, your physical presence at events is important for improving your word-of-mouth publicity. It offers you the opportunity to speak to readers (and potential readers) one on one.

- At events, you should create a comfortable environment where the audience can ask questions and interact with you.

- Always have copies of your books to sell and sign. You do not necessarily have to get the books sent to the venue beforehand if you are willing to transport them yourself, but if you don't have the means to bring copies to each venue, contact the owner and make sure it's okay to have copies sent ahead of time.

- If possible, try to make bookmarks or flyers advertising your social media and/or upcoming work.

- Book tours should be extensive, even aggressive. Twenty or thirty in-person events will generate more sales than just one or two.

- In his book *On Writing*, Stephen King says that "talent is cheaper than table salt. What separates the talented individual from the successful one is a lot of hard work."[11]

❧ Literary Citizenship

When you participate in the literary community for the sake of the greater good and advancing widely shared common interests, you are practicing literary citizenship. While we caution you against engaging in literary citizenship opportunistically, actions taken to benefit the whole community will ultimately benefit you as well, as an integral member of that community.

- **Champion small presses in your community** by reaching out to your local library and independent bookstores in your area and encouraging them to carry books by indie authors you love. If you're not sure how to find which library serves your community, visit this website: https://find-your-public-library.dp.la/. If you're not sure which indie bookstores serve your community, check here: https://www.indiebound.org/indie-bookstore-finder.

- **Teach books by indie authors you love.** Or, reach out to educators in your community and encourage them to use your favorite small press books in the classroom.

    Teachers who use small press texts in the classroom are not only helping their students gain a command of language. They are also helping indie authors find appreciative readers for their work, and creating community around that book. There is no greater gift a writer can receive.

    For educators who would like to teach Tupelo Press titles in their courses, we offer a range of complimentary curricular resources, which include lesson plans, writing assignments, reading lists, and poetry prompts. Many other publishers do the same. For more information about curricular resources, or to request a desk copy of a Tupelo Press book, please visit our course adoptions page: www.tupelopress.org/course-adoptions/.

❦ On the Value of Book Reviews

Book reviews can be a great way to build connections and relationships within the literary community. Here is a brief list of things that book reviews can accomplish for one's own craft and presence in the larger literary landscape:

- Book reviews can help literary presses and magazines become familiar with your work.

- Book reviews can help you build relationships with review editors. That way, when your book comes out, you have a working relationship with someone who can assign your book to a staff critic.

- Book reviews can help you build working relationships with authors in the literary community, particularly authors who are not in your same geographic area. This is wonderful if you're ever looking for someone to collaborate with for a reading, event, or AWP (Association of Writers & Writing Programs) panel, for example.

- Book reviews can help get your name in journals. And if you're interested in publishing in a prestigious journal, it's often easier to publish a review than a poem or story. This is because there's a reviewer shortage, while there's no shortage of writers submitting poems and stories. But once you've placed a review in the magazine, you have a working relationship with the editors and they'll likely be more receptive to a submission of creative work.

In general, book reviews are good karma. This is because they are a blessing to the authors and presses whose books you are reviewing. With that in mind, when your book or project comes to fruition people will generally remember that you supported others. This "good karma" makes individuals in the literary community excited to help you in your hour of need.

Retail and Distribution

While it is your publisher's job to handle the logistics of getting your book from the printer to store shelves, that doesn't mean you should avoid seeking out more venues for distribution. They might not know about your favorite local bookstore, and the store might be happy to carry a book by a local author. Knowing how to communicate with both local and regional distributors will improve your book's circulation and sales. This section will give you some ideas on how to make headway with retailers and other locations likely to offer your book.

☞ Location, Location, Location

All politics is local, right? Tip O'Neill's famous saying holds true even in the realm of book marketing. Searching for and playing off the similarities between you and your audience will bear out in sales. This means you should establish strong local connections and be aware of the local market climate. Are there booksellers in or around your town/city? Do they look for local authors to help sell and promote? Are there places nearby that host readings/signings? Get these people on your team. If you create a good name for yourself locally, you are that much closer to garnering regional and maybe even national attention.

Local independent bookstores are a good place to market your book. Many authors assume this is a difficult task, but don't be intimidated: Many local bookstores, especially independent ones, are more than happy to sell books by local authors. Generally, they have special stickers indicating works from local authors, if not entire sections devoted to local books and authors. A downside to smaller bookstores is they frequently ask for a consignment deal and pay for books once they are sold, rather than buying them in advance. In this case, it is still usually worthwhile to offer a small number of your books. To follow up, you should monitor the sales and determine whether to keep them there. Though you do not necessarily need to make an appointment to speak with a local bookstore manager for sales purposes, it is always a good idea to give the store a heads up. Be prepared with an invoice, in case the bookstore agrees to buy your book.

When working with small independent bookshops, go out of your way to provide them with everything they'll need, including display materials, extra book copies, promotional handouts, and anything else you can think of (giveaways are always great advertising anyway).

❦ Local Bookstores

- Establishing relationships with your local booksellers makes them much more likely to promote your books, especially independent shops who are less likely to be contacted by major publishers.

- You can also reach out to bookstores by sending letters or postcards asking them to reorder your book. Make sure the letters are personal, with correct information. Sellers are more likely to read handwritten letters.

- You can send newsletters to booksellers (as well as to your fans) to keep them informed of any new publicity or advertising.

❦ Libraries

- With proper handling, libraries are an incredibly useful market. Libraries buy from major jobbers and wholesalers, so you must first make sure your book is listed in their relevant databases. (Ingram is the most prominent.) There are four kinds of libraries: academic libraries that cater to colleges and universities; public libraries located in towns and cities; school libraries in K–12 school districts; and special libraries such as those found in prisons, hospitals, and museums. In total, there are nearly 124,000 libraries of all kinds in the United States.

- Because libraries cannot read or use everything they are sent, many subscribe to magazines or journals to get a better idea of the market (including *Choice, Library Journal, School Library Journal,* and *Publisher's Weekly*). These periodicals offer media kits and space for advertising. Consult each publication's website to get an idea of their individual practices, and be sure to accompany submissions with complete publication information including price, publication date, and ISBN.

❧ Cafés

- Cafés do not always sell books, but they make great locations for events and readings. If you're not sure you will be able to draw a large crowd, a local café is a good place to start, as they are usually small in size. It is almost always beneficial for small cafés to host author readings and they should be an easy location to secure. Most cafés will encourage you to bring any books you wish to sell to your reading or event. A good incentive to encourage the audience to purchase books is to offer to sign them after the reading.

- Some cafés also sell books regularly, though they lean toward used books over new. If you are scoping out an event location and come across a café that has books for sale, inquire further. Like local bookstores, they may ask you to sell on consignment or they may turn down your offer—either way, there is no harm in asking.

Events are a way of networking and connecting with people who are already interested in work like yours. Going to readings and attending other people's events are a great way to meet new people and form new connections with other authors and people interested in the literary world.

Live readings are especially important for poets, but they are also a great option for prose and hybrid writers. Readings, including online readings, are and always have been the best way to market poetry. Self-marketing by poets is particularly important today. Poetry is generally considered a niche market, which can make marketing both easier and harder for you. Though the market is smaller for poets than that of fiction writers, it may be more accessible. Depending on your location, it should be relatively easy to find a slam poetry venue. Though slam is not for everyone, it could be a good place to discover members of your audience. Sometimes readings and open mics accompany slam events. If slam *is* your style, it's a remarkable opportunity for you to read your work directly to that audience. Also, in the time a fiction writer reads an excerpt of their novel, a poet can recite several poems, giving the audience a much broader view of their work, a perk before purchase.

Declining an invitation to participate in an event may discourage the host/venue from asking again. Though it's impossible to say yes to everything, you should try to attend as many events as possible, especially local ones. Even if you're not being asked to participate, accept offers to sit in at events; they increase your chance to make casual connections with other authors and experts in your field. When you make new connections, consider suggesting an event together next time or inviting them to an upcoming event of yours. Similarly, don't be afraid to ask questions at the event, even as a guest. Asking questions could be your ticket to having your flyers displayed and your book advertised.

But what if you *aren't* getting invited to readings or events? Reach out! Get in contact with people and places known for hosting events and ask if they would consider hosting you. If you have the means, you could even host your own reading somewhere. Bottom line: Taking initiative and being creative pay off.

CHAPTER FOUR

The Publisher's Role

Once you are equipped to successfully self-promote, how can your publisher continue to support you in your efforts? As this guide has emphasized, an independent publisher's success is dependent upon the success of your book. This chapter highlights the specific resources your publisher might have to help you succeed, based on what we do at Tupelo Press.

A major portion of your publisher's resources are from the network they have created through the distribution and collection of awards, honors, reviews, and other media events. While striving to make your own connections as an indie author, planning and coordinating your marketing efforts with your publisher will allow the press to leverage these connections to your advantage. Maintain an open channel of communication with your publisher; alerting the press to major events (readings, signings, conferences, and other physical interactions/campaigns) will give them time to generate a larger buzz through their media networks.

❦ Author Questionnaires

Tupelo Press sends a questionnaire to new authors so we can better understand you as a person and the content of your work. Our Author Questionnaire goes a long way toward establishing your demographic for the press and guiding our marketing efforts. Your publisher may send you a similar questionnaire. Regardless of the format, the information you provide is invaluable to your publisher's marketing plans.

❦ Catalog

Every summer and winter, Tupelo sends out catalogs highlighting our newest releases to sales representatives and board members who will be influential in spreading information about new books through the industry. Tupelo also sends out emails and e-cards to everyone on our mailing list about upcoming news and exciting events. This is an excellent platform from which to advertise new books, as well as to highlight author interviews, awards, and buzz surrounding publications. If we happen to miss something like an interview or a review, authors can just email us to let us know and we'll post it on social media. Your publisher might have similar marketing practices, so always ask!

❧ Awards

Tupelo maintains extensive lists of literary prizes and awards, for which we nominate your book. They range from relatively small, local prize pools to large, prestigious literary honors such as the Pulitzer and the National Book Award. If you discover an applicable contest on your own for which your publisher has not nominated you, contact the press.

❧ Marketing

We noted at the end of Chapter 1 that usually publishers will "market your book for four months leading up to the book's release and typically for about a year afterwards." Of course, the timeline and what can be done change depending on the time of year, the specific content of your book, the geography of the publishing landscape, and other decisive factors. As a small press, Tupelo does what we can to adapt to the conditions around us rather than trying to influence them directly. But, for the sake of clarification, here are a few initiatives you can expect. As always, check in with your publisher and see what similar practices you can expect.

- Leading up to release, Tupelo sends out and manages the response to print galleys and galley letters to inspire course or retail adoption.

- After release, Tupelo sends out copies to individual reviewers and influential figures within the industry.

- Tupelo spreads news to our dedicated readership through our social media networks.

- Tupelo submits to as many post-publication awards as we're aware of and which are pertinent to your book (though you should still seek out more).

- If possible, Tupelo will engage in selective print and digital advertisements.

- Tupelo will help you equip yourself for conferences—talk to the press about getting more copies of your book.

Direct contact with your publisher is the best way to ensure both parties are meeting their obligations. Reach out when you're unsure of what you can do to help, and have faith in both your abilities and the work your press has done to bring the work of many authors into the mainstream.

CHAPTER FIVE

Advice from Tupelo's Authors

Y ou aren't the first author to struggle with marketing an un-
known book; Tupelo Press has helped hundreds of authors to
rise out of obscurity and into the public eye. The following list
collects the best advice that Tupelo authors wish to pass on to you, as
an author just starting out.

❦ Local Readings

When asked what strategies proved most effective in spreading the
word about their new publication, Tupelo's authors responded almost
unanimously that seeking out public reading opportunities was critical.

**Nancy Naomi Carlson, translator of *Stone Lyre:
Poems of René Char* and *Calazaza's Delicious Dereliction*:**

"Arranging local readings the first year the book came out
seemed to result in the most sales."

Natasha Sajé, author of *Bend* and *Vivarium*:

"When I was younger, I turned down offers to read if they
didn't pay or I had to pay for my travel. Now that I'm not as
strapped for money, I wish I had not done that . . . [L]ook at
the long-term benefit, think of travel as tax-deductible, as time
that's an investment in your career."

**David Huddle, author of *My Immaculate Assassin*, *Hazel*,
and *The Faulkes Chronicle*:**

"I make an effort to get readings at bookstores, colleges, and
private schools."

Ruth Ellen Kocher, author of *Third Voice* and *domina Un/blued*:

"You shouldn't be afraid to contact venues and ask if they would like to schedule a reading. Young writers sometimes feel as though they need to wait for an invitation from a large venue or a university reading series. It not only doesn't hurt to ask but it's also helpful to offer. Many university reading series are underfunded and can't pay large honorariums to familiar names. You never know when you're exactly what a series is looking for."

Lee Sharkey, author of *Calendars of Fire* and *Walking Backwards*:

"It used to be I sought out reading dates in any library, bookstore, or reading series that would have me. I might travel 100 miles or more and wind up reading to a handful of people, none of whom had the slightest inclination to buy a poetry book. These days I suss out reading venues with the aim of scheduling readings in places that are likely to draw a substantial audience of folks who love poetry and understand the importance of supporting poets and publishers in their work. Scheduling readings strategically leaves me time to promote the readings I do give thoroughly and keeps me from burning out."

❦ Book Launch Parties

Creating an event that an audience can associate with your work is another highly effective method for generating buzz and spreading word-of-mouth publicity. Your book launch can be either in-person or virtual. Associating your book with a good party where audience members can meet each other in the context of your work creates a sense of community. You likely have friends, colleagues, and family in dozens of cities across the country. With their help and sponsorship, organize launch parties in as many towns and cities as possible, both in person and online through the magic of Zoom, Google Meet, or Skype.

Nancy Naomi Carlson:

"I recommend holding a book launch party when the book first comes out, with good food and fellowship."

✾ Reach Out to Friends

Your friends and family want to see you succeed. Finding those who will enjoy your book and introducing them to your work can be just as important as collecting a following online.

David Huddle:

"I send copies of my books to friends who may be inclined to buy books for their friends and/or to recommend my book to others."

✾ Don't Be Afraid of the Internet

Several chapters in this book have already emphasized the importance of online social networking. Tupelo's authors offer a few tips from their own experience.

Elena Karina Byrne, author of *The Flammable Bird* and *Masque*:

"I think I barely did any PR at all for my first book *Flammable Bird* with Zoo Press . . . I can say I have finally come on board with social media, because of my daughter and Omnidawn [Publishing], so Facebook, Twitter, and Instagram are really helping . . . Even the 'famous' poets seem to do it. I do email blasts with photos as well . . . [I]t's hard as a new author to promote oneself, but by the third book one realizes you have to if you want to sell some books! I sold out in my first reading so maybe it works. Reaching out to individual friends is a nice thing . . . I have also given away books to friends and mentors."

Lee Sharkey:

"Over the months before *Calendars of Fire* and *Walking Backwards* appeared, I compiled email lists of over 600 friends and friends-in-poetry and designed email book announcements that featured a picture of the cover along with a link to the Tupelo website and info about reading dates. As soon as the books came out, I mailed the announcements. Whereas Facebook posts elicited lots of 'likes,' the email announcements resulted in full and generous responses, many from people I hadn't been in contact with in years, and a flurry of traffic on the Tupelo website."

☙ Exploit Word of Mouth

You are perfectly capable of generating buzz by connecting with other individuals in unexpected times and places. Although this book encourages you to plan ahead and think about the bigger picture, don't forget about connecting with the people you encounter every day.

Lee Sharkey:

"I recommend printing postcards with your book cover on the front and a blurb and contact info for Tupelo on the back. I carry these with me wherever I go to give out when the occasion arises to invite someone to a reading (I scribble the date and place on the back), or just remind them that they might want to order the book."

CHAPTER SIX

Conclusions

I f you take nothing else away from this guide, understand that your participation in marketing your book is vital. To get your book sold, your publisher requires your resourcefulness and drive. As an author, you need to go out and make connections, form relationships, and always maintain the work you have done by keeping your audience updated. Include your publisher in your audience—be sure to let them know who you are working with, the events you are attending, and the techniques you are employing so that the press can adapt their own strategies. Remember, you are your own best salesperson. By working together with your publisher, your words have power to resonate throughout the literary and academic worlds.

Set your goals. Envision what ultimate success looks like for you, then establish and prioritize the individual goals that will get you there. Be selective in choosing the opportunities presented to you; always make decisions based on your goals. If a given opportunity does not align with your goals, avoid it.

Create a budget that works for you—for your wallet, your calendar, and your expectations. The amount of time and money you can invest will inform your expectations of success. Your actual success is best measured by how well you budget yourself. Make sure your schedule and your budget line up with your goals realistically.

Define your target market. This is the group of people who will purchase your book. Once you understand the distinct features of this group, connect with them in genuine, exciting ways, through book signings, webinars, or whatever community interaction is possible. Knowing your audience from the inside out will help you to effectively reach them, making your marketing less costly and infinitely more rewarding.

Be judicious. Instead of trying every social media website on the Internet, use only ones that appeal to you, your brand, and your lifestyle. Instead of attending every event you get invited to, select those that maximize opportunities for networking and sales. Instead of shouting about your work at every given opportunity, let it come up naturally in conversation with others. As with words, choose your time, money, and connections carefully.

Keep your outlets updated. A well-updated website is a well-updated audience. Be sure that anything new going on with you as an author and any news pertinent to your book is accessible. Avoid long periods of inactivity—post regular content to keep a consistent online readership.

Long-term marketing. You can use the revenue you have earned to reinvest in the marketing of your book. Now that your book is selling, look at how you can use the income you have made and continue to make to further increase its visibility. That will likely involve an assessment of your advertising and marketing techniques to determine which are the most effective.

Measure your book's success beyond book sales. Consider the book's impact on the rest of your business. If your book is nonfiction and is at least partly designed to promote a service you offer, it might prove a success regardless of how well it sells. Joanna Penn, author of *How to Find Your Vital Vocation,* was not actively seeking more coaching work, but since her book came out, inquiries for her coaching have more than quadrupled.

Follow your instincts, they got you this far. Remember that while publishing, promoting, and marketing a book, a lot can happen. Give yourself time to prepare and be ready for each challenge as it comes.

The future of your book rests in your hands. Even though it is published or in production, there are still decisions to be made and lessons to be learned. Although marketing your book is an ongoing learning process, we hope that this guide helps you to feel more confident and prepared. Remember that this is a collaborative process, and your publishing team is always there to help.

You're ready to take on this next chapter—just think, you already wrote a whole soon-to-be-published book! You can be confident that independent and university publishers are excited to work with you on getting your books out into the world and in the hands of fond, dedicated readers.

Review, Interview, and Submission Directory

The Adirondack Review

"The Adirondack Review is an online quarterly magazine of art and literature. We publish poetry, fiction, translation, essays, interviews, and reviews, plus a full slate of art and photography per issue."

Contact Information and Submission Guidelines
http://adirondackreview.homestead.com/submissions.html

Agni

"The website grows biweekly with postings of new online-only fiction, poetry, essays, reviews, and interviews."

Contact Information and Submission Guidelines
www.bu.edu/agni/essays/print/2004/59-birkerts.html

AGNI Magazine
Boston University
236 Bay State Road
Boston, MA 02215

American Literary Review

"The American Literary Review welcomes submissions of previously unpublished poems, short stories, and creative non-fiction. Simultaneous submissions are acceptable if noted in your cover letter."

Contact Information and Submission Guidelines
https://americanliteraryreview.submittable.com/

University of North Texas
1155 Union Circle #311307
Denton, TX 76203
americanliteraryreview@gmail.com

American Microreviews & Interviews

"American Microreviews and Interviews started in 2013. The site exists to promote books, authors, journals, and presses we believe in. All posts are considered the property of individual contributors."

Contact Information and Submission Guidelines
www.americanmicroreviews.com/about

Barn Owl Review

"Barn Owl Review is an independent literary magazine dedicated to publishing the highest quality poetry from both emerging and established writers."

Contact Information and Submission Guidelines

www.barnowlreview.com/Submissions.html

The Bind

"The Bind was created to increase readership for new poetry books by women and non-binary authors. We publish creative reviews of full-length collections and chapbooks of poetry and hybrid-genre work, including translated work."

Contact Information and Submission Guidelines

www.thebind.net/about

Big Other

Reviews of small and independent press titles.

Contact Information and Submission Guidelines

https://bigother.com/submit/

Boxcar Poetry Review

"Boxcar Poetry Review is an online poetry journal showcasing the work of new and established poets with new issues appearing quarterly."

Contact Information and Submission Guidelines

www.boxcarpoetry.com/submissions.html

Cloudy House

"Though project books have a long history, they currently enjoy unprecedented popularity in the MFA thesis classroom and on the publication circuit. But what makes a book of poetry a project book, and what separates a successful project from an unsuccessful one? How does taking on a project affect a poet's writing process, and what does the proliferation of project books in general signify for contemporary poetry? Poets Cynthia Marie Hoffman and Nick Lantz created the Cloudy House as a forum for answering these questions and exploring multiple perspectives on the project book phenomenon."

Contact Information and Submission Guidelines

www.thecloudyhouse.com/

The Collagist

"The Collagist is published once every two months. Each issue features original fiction, poetry, and essays, most of which come from unsolicited submissions."

Contact Information and Submission Guidelines

http://thecollagist.com/collagistsubmissions/

The Colorado Review & Colorado Review Editors Blog

"We consider short fiction and personal essays with contemporary themes (no genre fiction or literary criticism)."

Contact Information and Submission Guidelines:

http://coloradoreview.colostate.edu/colorado-review/submit/

Book Review Guidelines:

https://coloradoreview.colostate.edu/wp-content/uploads/2019/11/Book-Review-Guidelines.pdf

Colorado State University
9105 Campus Delivery
Fort Collins, Colorado 80523-9105

Columbia Poetry Review

"Now in its twenty-seventh year, Columbia Poetry Review is published annually by Columbia College Chicago's Department of Creative Writing. It is a student-edited, nationally distributed literary journal."

Contact Information and Submission Guidelines

www.colum.edu/columbiapoetryreview/submissions.php

Columbia Poetry Review
Department of Creative Writing
Columbia College Chicago
600 South Michigan Avenue
Chicago, IL 60605

Connotation Press

"Connotation Press accepts submissions in poetry, fiction, creative nonfiction, play writing, screenplay, interview, book review, music review, video (for spoken word or music or ...), etc. Basically, we're looking at virtually every genre or crossover genre you can create."

Contact Information and Submission Guidelines

www.connotationpress.com

The Critical Flame

"Founded in late 2008, the mission of The Critical Flame is simple: to encourage intelligent public discussion about literature and culture through long-form literary and critical essays covering a wide range of topics."

Contact Information and Submission Guidelines

http://criticalflame.org/contact-submit/

decomP Magazine

"Formerly known as Decomposition Magazine, decomP (ISSN: 1947-0436) is an online, bimonthly, literary magazine that was founded in April 2004 by Mike Smith."

Contact Information and Submission Guidelines

www.decompmagazine.com/submit.htm

Denver Quarterly

"Unsolicited manuscripts of fiction, essays, interviews, reviews, and poetry are welcomed from October 15 to February 15. We ask that you wait to hear back from us regarding your current submission before sending another piece of writing."

Contact Information and Submission Guidelines

www.du.edu/denverquarterly/submissions/

Denver Quarterly
University of Denver
Department of English
2000 E Asbury
Denver, CO 80208

Diagram

"As our name indicates, we're interested in representations. In naming. In indicating. In schematics. In the labelling and taxonomy of things. In poems that masquerade as stories; in stories that disguise themselves as indices or obituaries."

Contact Information and Submission Guidelines

Submission Guidelines:
http://thediagram.com/subs.html

Book Reviews:
http://thediagram.com/reviews.html

DIAGRAM Reviews
c/o Lawrence Lenhart
Dept of English, PO Box 6032
Northern Arizona University
Flagstaff, AZ 86011

Dressing Room Poetry Journal

Contact Information and Submission Guidelines

www.dressingroompoetryjournal.com
/submissions.html

Fjords Review

"Fjords Review is edited by Miguel Pichardo. The internationally distributed newsstand magazine with a weekly online component was founded in 2010 by John Gosslee, who was editor and chief until 2016."

Contact Information and Submission Guidelines

www.fjordsreview.com/
https://fjordsreview.submittable.com/submit

Gazing Grain Press

"Gazing Grain Press is an inclusive feminist literary press staffed by alumni of the George Mason University creative writing MFA program. Each year, the press publishes a chapbook of poems and a chapbook of prose, with a special emphasis on hybrid work."

Contact Information and Submission Guidelines

www.gazinggrainpress.com/guidelines

Gigantic Sequins

"Our editors like to publish writers & artists who have their hands in various sorts of figurative creative cookie jars, as well as writers & artists at a variety of different stages in their careers."

Contact Information and Submission Guidelines

www.giganticsequins.com/submit.html

Hiram Poetry Review

"The Hiram Poetry Review is published annually by the English Department at Hiram College in Hiram, Ohio."

Contact Information and Submission Guidelines

https://hirampoetryreview.wordpress.com
/submissions/

Hiram Poetry Review
P.O. Box 162
Hiram, Ohio 44234

JMWW

"jmww is a literary journal publishing fiction, flash, poetry, essays, interviews, book reviews, and other miscellany weekly."

Contact Information and Submission Guidelines

www.jmww.submittable.com/submit

Kenyon Review

"Today, KR is devoted to nurturing, publishing, and celebrating the best in contemporary writing. We're expanding the community of diverse readers and writers, across the globe, at every stage of their lives."

Contact Information and Submission Guidelines

www.kenyonreview.org/submission/

Finn House
102 W. Wiggin St
Kenyon College
Gambier, OH 43022-9623

Les Femmes Folles

"Les Femmes Folles (LFF) is an organization around the online journal supporting women in art founded and curated by Sally Deskins."

Contact Information and Submission Guidelines

http://femmesfollesnebraska.tumblr.com/callforart-writing

The Literary Review

"The Literary Review (TLR) publishes the best new fiction, poetry, and prose from a broad community of international writers and translators, both emerging and established, whose commonality is literary quality and urgency of voice and artistic conviction."

Contact Information and Submission Guidelines

www.theliteraryreview.org/submit/

Fairleigh Dickinson University
49 South Passaic Avenue, B2
Chatham, NJ 07928

The Lit Pub

"Recommendations come in all shapes and sizes. Some of our contributors submit cute, quirky lists of reasons why they think a book deserves more attention. Other contributors submit serious, critical analyses with a more academic tone."

Contact Information and Submission Guidelines

https://thelitpub.submittable.com/submit/11136/submit-your-book-recommendation-here

5550 Laura Lane
Lorain, OH 44053

The Los Angeles Review and Los Angeles Review of Books Blog

"The Los Angeles Review, an annual print and online literary journal established in 2003, is the voice of Los Angeles, and the voice of the nation."

Contact Information and Submission Guidelines

Submission Guidelines
http://losangelesreview.org/submission/

Book Reviews
http://blog.lareviewofbooks.org/

6671 Sunset Blvd., Suite 1521
Los Angeles, CA 90028

Newpages

"Calls for writing, art, book-length manuscripts, photography, and more from magazines, publishers, writing conferences and events, writing programs, etc."

Contact Information and Submission Guidelines

www.newpages.com/classifieds/calls-for-submissions

PO Box 1580
Bay City, MI 48706

The Nervous Breakdown

"The Nervous Breakdown features the work of published and emerging authors and poets from around the world."

Contact Information and Submission Guidelines

http://thenervousbreakdown.com/submissions/

PANK Magazine

"Founded in 2006 by M. Bartley Seigel and Roxane Gay, PANK Magazine is a literary magazine fostering access to emerging and innovative poetry and prose, publishing the brightest and most promising writers for the most adventurous readers."

Contact Information and Submission Guidelines

https://pankmagazine.com/submit-2/

The Pedestal

"As editors of The Pedestal Magazine, we intend to support both established and burgeoning writers. We are committed to promoting artistic diversity and celebrating the voice of the individual."

Contact Information and Submission Guidelines

www.thepedestalmagazine.com/submissions/

Pleiades Review of Books

"Please note: not all sent books will be reviewed, though we do review 40+ books in each issue."

Contact Information and Submission Guidelines

www.pleiadesmag.com/submit/

Pleiades Book Review
Dept of English, Martin 336
University of Central Missouri
Warrensburg, MO 64093

Ploughshares Blog

"Ploughshares has published quality literature since 1971. Best known for our award-winning Ploughshares literary journal, we also publish Ploughshares Solos—digital-first long stories and essays—and a lively literary blog. Since 1989, we have been based at Emerson College in downtown Boston."

Contact Information and Submission Guidelines

www.pshares.org/submit/journal/guidelines

Emerson College
120 Boylston St.
Boston, MA 02116

Rob McLennan's Blog

Poet, writer, and editor McLennan blogs extensively about poetry, fiction, and nonfiction.

Contact Information and Submission Guidelines

http://robmclennan.blogspot.com/

The Rumpus

"The Rumpus is a place where people come to be themselves through their writing, to tell their stories or speak their minds in the most artful and authentic way they know how, and to invite each of you, as readers, commenters, or future contributors, to do the same."

Contact Information and Submission Guidelines

http://therumpus.net/about/#Writers Guidelines

846 19th St.
Des Moines IA 50314

Stirring: A Literary Collection

"Our goal is to elevate writing and art. We like to see creative work from all writing genres and a variety of visual art media."

Contact Information and Submission Guidelines

www.stirringlit.com/submit/

Sundog Lit

"Since 2012, Sundog Lit has featured the very best in fiction, poetry, nonfiction, and art online. With each issue, we strive to bring readers work that sings, cracks, pumps, breaks, loves, and wails."

Contact Information and Submission Guidelines

https://sundoglit.com/submissions/

Tarpaulin Sky

"As with Tarpaulin Sky's books, the magazine focuses on cross-genre / trans-genre / hybrid forms as well as innovative poetry and prose."

Contact Information and Submission Guidelines

https://tarpaulinsky.com/

https://tarpaulinsky.com/info2/submission-guidelines/

THEThe Poetry

"THEthe Poetry is a blog about poetics, for both poets and non-poets."

Contact Information and Submission Guidelines

www.thethepoetry.com/about/

The Volta

"Please send us finished books or bound galleys of forthcoming titles."

Contact Information and Submission Guidelines

thevolta.org/thevolta-submissions.html

Housten Donham, Editor
Univ. of AZ, Dept. of English
1423 E. University Blvd.
Modern Languages Bldg., Rm. 445
Tucson, AZ 85721

Up the Staircase Quarterly

"Established in March 2008, Up the Staircase Quarterly is an online journal of poetry, art, interviews, and reviews."

Contact Information and Submission Guidelines

www.upthestaircase.org/submit.html

Word For/Word

"Word For/ Word is open to all types of poetry, prose and visual art, but prefers innovative and post-avant work with an astute awareness of the materials, rhythms, trajectories and emerging forms of the contemporary."

Contact Information and Submission Guidelines

http://www.wordforword.info

WordMothers

"WordMothers aspires to introduce female-identifying writers to new readers, inspire other writers, engage with book industry professionals, and encourage fresh dialogue concerning the role of women in the literary arts today."

Contact Information and Submission Guidelines

https://wordmothers.com/

Writer's Digest Poetic Asides

"Are you passionate about writing poetry? Check out Robert Lee Brewer's blog, Poetic Asides. You'll find poetry prompts, solid tips on writing poetry, interviews with poets, and blog posts highlighting poetic forms like chant, haibun or nonet poems, rispetto, and prose poetry."

Contact Information and Submission Guidelines

http://www.writersdigest.com/editor-blogs/poetic-asides

1500 Eryn Circle
Suwanee GA 30024

Notes

1   The National Opinion Research Center, *Poetry in America* (University of Chicago Press, 2006).

2   www.theguardian.com/books/2018/sep/17/us-losing-appetite-for-reading-fiction-research-finds, *Guardian*, September 17, 2018.

3   Nielsen Global Survey of Trust in Advertising, "Under the Influence: Consumer Trust in Advertising," September 17, 2013, www.nielsen.com/us/en/insights/article/2013/under-the-influence-consumer-trust-in-advertising/.

4   Kimberly A. Whitler, "Why Word of Mouth Marketing Is the Most Important Social Media," *Forbes*, July 17, 2014, www.forbes.com/sites/kimberlywhitler/2014/07/17/why-word-of-mouth-marketing-is-the-most-important-social-media/#6e3abf2a54a8.

5   Ibid.

6   Gertrude Stein, *Three Lives; and Q.E.D.: Authoritative Texts, Contexts, Criticism*, ed. Marianne DeKoven (New York: W. W. Norton, 2006).

7   See https://www.huffpost.com/entry/making-my-case-why-author_b_5708455.

8   Andrew Perrin and Maeve Duggan, "Americans' Internet Access: 2000–2015," Pew Research Center, June 26, 2015, www.pewresearch.org/internet/2015/06/26/americans-internet-access-2000-2015/.

9   Fauzia Burke. *Online Marketing for Busy Authors: A Step-by-step Guide* (Berrett-Koehler, 2016).

10 National Opinion Research Center, *Poetry in America*.

11 Stephen King, *On Writing: A Memoir on the Craft* (Simon and Schuster, 2000).

Index